an Adriana Rosales Brand

Gratitude
JOURNAL ~*Pro*

Daily Planning, Weekly Planner & Budget Sheets

ROSALES MAVERICKS PUBLISHING STUDIO

Copyright © 2021 Rosales Mavericks Publishing Studio & Adriana & Company™
All rights reserved. No part of this publication may be reproduced, distributed, or transmitted in any form or by any means, including photocopying, recording, or other electronic or mechanical methods, without the prior written permission of the publisher, except in the case of brief quotations embodied in critical reviews and certain other noncommercial uses permitted by copyright law. For permission requests, write to the publisher, addressed "Attention: Latinas 100,"
at the address below.
ISBN: 9798712108671
Find out more about our Latinas 100 Writers Community.
Publish your story in our next anthology for FREE.
Front cover image by Adriana Rosales
Book design by Designer Adriana Rosales
Printed in the United States of America.
First printing edition 2021
Rosales Mavericks Publishing Studio
1180 N. Town Center Suite #100
Las Vegas, Nevada 89144
www.Latinas100.com
www.Adriana.Company/PublishingStudio

Why cultivate a Gratitude Practice?

A gratitude practice is the key to becoming what you have wanted to become all along.

When you show appreciation for the things, people, places and experiences that make up your life, the Universe allows for more positive energy to shift your way.

Being grateful for what you have now means that you recognize and acknowledge how fortunate and blessed you are.

It is important to show this appreciation in your everyday life. There is no need to wait for a life-changing event to finally realize how blessed you truly are. The time is now!

By having a consistent gratitude practice you will be able to experience more joy, live calmly, and feel more motivated.

In the following 90 days, you have the opportunity to build the foundation for your gratitude practice. Research suggests that it takes 21 days to build or break a habit and it takes 90 days to create a lifestyle.

So, what are you waiting for?

This journal was designed to help guide your practice by providing a daily prompt, which will make it easier for you to make gratitude a consistent part of your lifestyle.

Your moment of transformation and renewal starts now!

This Journal also has room for out of the blue journaling ideas and finance prompts and daily and weekly pages. It's intended for an all in one experience. Enjoy!

DAILY GRATITUDE PRACTICE

DATE: _____

Write a few sentences describing what is something about your health that you are grateful for.

Daily Inspiration

Gratitude opens the door to the power, the wisdom, the creativity of the Universe. You open the door through gratitude.

-Deepak Chopra-

DAILY GRATITUDE PRACTICE

DATE: _____

Write a few sentences describing one of your favourite memories that you are thankful for.

Daily Inspiration

The more you praise and celebrate your life, the more there is in life to celebrate.

-Oprah Winfrey-

DAILY GRATITUDE PRACTICE

DATE: _____

Write a few sentences describing one thing that starts with the letter A that you are grateful for.

Daily Inspiration

Be grateful for what you have, and where you are in your journey. Gratitude is key to manifesting abundance.

-Abraham Hicks-

DAILY GRATITUDE PRACTICE

DATE: _____

Write a few sentences describing one friend, that you greatly appreciate, that is part of your life.

Daily Inspiration

We should all be thankful for those people who rekindle our inner spirit.

-Albert Schweitzery-

DAILY GRATITUDE PRACTICE

DATE: _____

Write a few sentences describing something in your room that you are grateful to have, and briefly explain how it makes you feel.

Daily Inspiration

What a precious privilege it is to be alive – to breathe, to think, to enjoy, to love.

-Marcus Aurelius-

DAILY GRATITUDE PRACTICE

DATE: _____

Write a few sentences describing one thing that starts with the letter B that you are grateful for.

Daily Inspiration

Happiness is the spiritual experience of living every minute with love, grace, and gratitude.

-Denis Waitley-

DAILY GRATITUDE PRACTICE

DATE: _____

Write a few sentences describing one thing in your home that you greatly appreciate having and that brings you joy.

Daily Inspiration

Gratitude is the single most important ingredient to living a successful and fulfilled life.

-Jack Canfield-

DAILY GRATITUDE PRACTICE

DATE: _____

Write a few sentences describing something about your current job/profession that you are grateful for.

Daily Inspiration

When we are grateful, life gives us even more reasons to be grateful.

-LaTisha Cotto-

DAILY GRATITUDE PRACTICE

DATE: _____

Write a few sentences describing one thing that starts with the letter C that you are grateful for.

Daily Inspiration

Wear gratitude like a cloak and it will feed every corner of your life.

-Rumi-

DAILY GRATITUDE PRACTICE

DATE: _____

Write a few sentences describing a family member you are grateful for.

Daily Inspiration

Gratitude is a powerful catalyst for happiness. It's the spark that lights a fire of joy in your soul.

-Amy Collette-

DAILY GRATITUDE PRACTICE

DATE: _____

Write a few sentences describing why you are thankful for your pet.

Daily Inspiration

Gratitude will shift you to a higher frequency, and you will attract much better things.

-Rhonda Byrne-

DAILY GRATITUDE PRACTICE

DATE: _____

Write a few sentences describing one thing that starts with the letter D that you are grateful for.

Daily Inspiration

Gratitude helps you to grow and expand; it brings joy and laughter into your life and into the lives of those around you.

-Eileen Caddy-

DAILY GRATITUDE PRACTICE

DATE: _____

Write a few sentences describing a difficult moment that you overcame and explain how grateful you feel for the lessons learned.

Daily Inspiration

Gratitude makes sense of our past, brings peace for today, and creates a vision for tomorrow.

-Melody Beattie-

DAILY GRATITUDE PRACTICE

DATE: _____

Write a few sentences describing how grateful you are for waking up and one thing you hope to accomplish throughout the day.

Daily Inspiration

If there is gratitude in your heart, then there will be tremendous sweetness in your eyes.

-Sri Chinmoy-

DAILY GRATITUDE PRACTICE

DATE: _____

Write a few sentences describing one thing that starts with the letter E that you are grateful for.

Daily Inspiration

The more grateful I am, the more beauty I see.

-Mary Davis-

DAILY GRATITUDE PRACTICE

DATE: _____

Write a few sentences describing how thankful and blessed you feel for having the body you have.

Daily Inspiration

Gratitude for the present moment and the fullness of life now is the true prosperity.

-Eckhart Tolle-

DAILY GRATITUDE PRACTICE

DATE: _____

Write a few sentences describing your favourite hobby. Explain how it brings you joy and how much you appreciate doing it.

Daily Inspiration

Gratitude is an antidote to negative emotions, a neutralizer of envy, hostility, worry, and irritation.

-Sonja Lyubomirsky-

DAILY GRATITUDE PRACTICE

DATE: _____

Write a few sentences describing one thing that starts with the letter F that you are grateful for.

Daily Inspiration

Thanks are the highest form of thought; and gratitude is happiness doubled by wonder.

-G.K. Chesterton-

DAILY GRATITUDE PRACTICE

DATE: _____

Write a few sentences describing one personality trait you are thankful for having.

Daily Inspiration

Once you begin to take note of the things you are grateful for, you begin to lose sight of the things that you lack.

-Germany Kent-

DAILY GRATITUDE PRACTICE

DATE: _____

Write a few sentences describing one happy memory from your childhood you are grateful for.

Daily Inspiration

Cultivate the habit of being grateful for every good thing that comes to you, and to give thanks continuously.

-Ralph Waldo Emerson-

DAILY GRATITUDE PRACTICE

DATE: _____

Write a few sentences describing one thing that starts with the letter G that you are grateful for.

Daily Inspiration

Let gratitude be the pillow upon which you kneel to say your nightly prayer.

-Maya Angelou-

DAILY GRATITUDE PRACTICE

DATE: _____

Write a few sentences describing a gift you are thankful to have received.

Daily Inspiration

The soul that gives thanks can find comfort in everything.

-Hannah Whitall Smith-

DAILY GRATITUDE PRACTICE

DATE: _____

Write a few sentences describing a teacher you greatly appreciate and that positively impacted your life.

Daily Inspiration

Gratitude bestows reverence...changing forever how we experience life and the world.

-John Milton-

DAILY GRATITUDE PRACTICE

DATE: _____

Write a few sentences describing one thing that starts with the letter H that you are grateful for.

Daily Inspiration

Appreciation can make a day, even change a life. Your willingness to put it into words is all that is necessary.

-Margaret Cousins-

DAILY GRATITUDE PRACTICE

DATE: _____

Write a few sentences describing a gesture you had with a stranger and how you experienced gratitude by being of service to others.

Daily Inspiration

Truly appreciate life, and you'll find that you have more of it.

-Ralph Marston-

DAILY GRATITUDE PRACTICE

DATE: _____

Write a few sentences describing a book you are grateful for reading.

Daily Inspiration

Whatever we are waiting for will surely come to us, but only when we are ready to receive it with an open and grateful heart.

-Sarah Ban Breathnach-

DAILY GRATITUDE PRACTICE

DATE: _____

Write a few sentences describing one thing that starts with the letter I that you are grateful for.

Daily Inspiration

Gratitude turns what we have into enough.

-Aesop-

DAILY GRATITUDE PRACTICE

DATE: _____

Write a few sentences describing 3 things you appreciate about your partner. If you are single, write 3 things about yourself.

Daily Inspiration

When we focus on our gratitude, the tide of disappointment goes out and the tide of love rushes in.

-Kristin Armstrong-

DAILY GRATITUDE PRACTICE

DATE: _____

Write a few sentences describing something you are grateful about your daily life.

Daily Inspiration

Gratitude unlocks all that's blocking us from really feeling truthful, really feeling authentic and vulnerable and happy.

-Gabrielle Bernstein-

DAILY GRATITUDE PRACTICE

DATE: _____

Write a few sentences describing one thing that starts with the letter J that you are grateful for.

Daily Inspiration

The thankful receiver bears a plentiful harvest.

-William Blake-

DAILY GRATITUDE PRACTICE

DATE: _____

Write a few sentences describing how grateful you are for sleeping on a soft, warm, and comfortable bed.

Daily Inspiration

Gratitude is one of the most medicinal emotions we can feel. It elevates our moods and fills us with joy.

-Sara Avant Stover-

DAILY GRATITUDE PRACTICE

DATE: _____

Write a few sentences describing a gesture someone had with you and briefly explain how much you appreciated it.

Daily Inspiration

No gesture is too small when done in gratitude.

-Oprah Winfrey-

DAILY GRATITUDE PRACTICE

DATE: _____

Write a few sentences describing one thing that starts with the letter K that you are grateful for.

Daily Inspiration

Gratitude is a state of being.

-Iyanla Vanzant-

DAILY GRATITUDE PRACTICE

DATE: _____

Write a few sentences describing five small things you usually take for granted. Reflect on how fortunate you are for having them.

Daily Inspiration

The miracle of gratitude is that it shifts your perception to such an extent that it changes the world you see.

-Dr. Robert Holden-

DAILY GRATITUDE PRACTICE

DATE: _____

Write a few sentences describing something great that happened to you last year. Explain how grateful you are for that experience.

Daily Inspiration

Living in a state of gratitude is the gateway to grace.

-Arianna Huffington-

DAILY GRATITUDE PRACTICE

DATE: _____

Write a few sentences describing one thing that starts with the letter L that you are grateful for.

Daily Inspiration

It's important to pause every now and then to appreciate all that we have, on every level.

-Shakti Gawain-

DAILY GRATITUDE PRACTICE

DATE: _____

Write a few sentences describing a fun activity or favourite hobby you are grateful for.

Daily Inspiration

Gratitude can transform common days into thanksgiving... and change ordinary opportunities into blessings.

-William Arthur Ward-

DAILY GRATITUDE PRACTICE

DATE: _____

Write a few sentences describing how appreciative you are of having a place to live.

Daily Inspiration

If you want to turn your life around, try thankfulness. It will change your life mightily.

-Gerald Good-

DAILY GRATITUDE PRACTICE

DATE: _____

Write a few sentences describing one thing that starts with the letter M that you are grateful for.

Daily Inspiration

Practice appreciation for who you are and what you have... and allow your life to unfold in the most amazing way.

-Millen Livis-

DAILY GRATITUDE PRACTICE

DATE: _____

Write a few sentences describing something that you are grateful for having today that you didn't have a year ago.

Daily Inspiration

When gratitude becomes an essential foundation in our lives, miracles start to appear everywhere.

-Emmanuel Dalgher-

DAILY GRATITUDE PRACTICE

DATE: _____

Write a few sentences describing one place you are grateful to have visited.

Daily Inspiration

Just keep saying thank you, forever and sincerely, for as long as we have voices.

-Elizabeth Gilbert-

DAILY GRATITUDE PRACTICE

DATE: _____

Write a few sentences describing one thing that starts with the letter N that you are grateful for.

Daily Inspiration

To be grateful is to find blessings in everything. This is the most powerful attitude to adopt, for there are blessings in everything.

-Alan Cohen-

DAILY GRATITUDE PRACTICE

DATE: _____

Write a few sentences describing the street you live in. What is something you see outside that you are grateful for?

Daily Inspiration

When life is sweet, say thank you and celebrate. And when life is bitter, say thank you and grow.

-Shauna Niequist-

DAILY GRATITUDE PRACTICE

DATE: _____

Write a few sentences describing a song that lifts up your mood and explain how grateful you are for it.

Daily Inspiration

Being thankful isn't always experienced as a natural state of existence, we must work at it like strength training for the heart.

-Larissa Gomez-

DAILY GRATITUDE PRACTICE

DATE: _____

Write a few sentences describing one thing that starts with the letter O that you are grateful for.

Daily Inspiration

Gratitude is the state of mind of thankfulness. As it's cultivated, we experience sympathetic joy: happiness at another's happiness.

-Stephen Levine-

DAILY GRATITUDE PRACTICE

DATE: _____

Write a few sentences describing a small luxury you bought and how grateful you are for having the opportunity to treat yourself.

Daily Inspiration

The longer you linger in gratitude, the more you draw your new life to you. For gratitude is the ultimate state of receivership.

-Dr. Joe Dispenza-

DAILY GRATITUDE PRACTICE

DATE: _____

Write a few sentences describing how thankful you are for being able to exercise and move your body.

Daily Inspiration

You want to become a better person? Just give thanks. Give thanks for all of it.

-Kamand Kojouri-

DAILY GRATITUDE PRACTICE

DATE: _____

Write a few sentences describing one thing that starts with the letter P that you are grateful for.

Daily Inspiration

When I started counting my blessings, my whole life turned around.

-Willie Nelson-

DAILY GRATITUDE PRACTICE

DATE: _____

Write a few sentences describing how grateful you are for the food you eat.

Daily Inspiration

Focusing on one thing that you are grateful for increases the energy of gratitude and rises the joy inside yourself.

-Oprah Winfrey-

DAILY GRATITUDE PRACTICE

DATE: _____

Write a few sentences describing your favourite self-care activity. Reflect on how much you appreciate having the time to relax.

Daily Inspiration

Gratitude paints little smiley faces on everything it touches.

-Richelle E. Goodrich-

DAILY GRATITUDE PRACTICE

DATE: _____

Write a few sentences describing one thing that starts with the letter Q that you are grateful for.

Daily Inspiration

Gratitude is a fuel, a medicine, and spiritual and emotional nourishment.

-Steve Maraboli-

DAILY GRATITUDE PRACTICE

DATE: _____

Write a few sentences describing one of your favourite parts inside your house and how grateful you feel for having that space.

Daily Inspiration

Even in the trials of life, if we have eyes to see them, we can find good things everywhere we look.

-Joanna Gaines-

DAILY GRATITUDE PRACTICE

DATE: _____

Write a few sentences describing three things you appreciate about the weather today.

Daily Inspiration

Gratitude is the inward feeling of kindness received.
Thankfulness is the natural impulse to express that feeling.

-Henry van Dyke-

DAILY GRATITUDE PRACTICE

DATE: _____

Write a few sentences describing one thing that starts with the letter R that you are grateful for.

Daily Inspiration

Gratitude is the closest thing to beauty manifested in an emotion.

-Mindy Kalin-

DAILY GRATITUDE PRACTICE

DATE: _____

Write a few sentences describing five things you are grateful about the city or town you live in.

Daily Inspiration

Be grateful for what you have and be ready to share it when the time comes.

-Michelle Obama-

DAILY GRATITUDE PRACTICE

DATE: _____

Write a few sentences describing three people you are thankful to have in your life.

Daily Inspiration

People who take the time to focus on the things they are grateful for are happier and healthier.

-Sheryl Sandberg-

DAILY GRATITUDE PRACTICE

DATE: _____

Write a few sentences describing one thing that starts with the letter S that you are grateful for.

Daily Inspiration

Once you feel grateful, you are in an energy that can create miracles.

-Joe Vitale-

DAILY GRATITUDE PRACTICE

DATE: _____

Write a few sentences describing three skills or abilities you are grateful to have.

Daily Inspiration

The grateful mind is constantly fixed upon the best. Therefore it tends to become the best.

-Wallace Wattles-

DAILY GRATITUDE PRACTICE

DATE: _____

Write a few sentences describing something unique about yourself you are grateful for.

Daily Inspiration

Something so simple, but it's important to take the time out from living and just appreciate what you've got right in front of you.

-L.A. Fiore-

DAILY GRATITUDE PRACTICE

DATE: _____

Write a few sentences describing one thing that starts with the letter T that you are grateful for.

Daily Inspiration

Gratitude can transform any situation. It alters your vibration, moving you from negative energy to positive.

-Oprah Winfrey-

DAILY GRATITUDE PRACTICE

DATE: _____

Write a few sentences describing a person you don't see very often but are grateful to have in your life.

Daily Inspiration

If you look hard enough, you will find that even tough times offer pearls worthy of gratitude.

-Richelle E. Goodrich-

DAILY GRATITUDE PRACTICE

DATE: _____

Write a few sentences describing how much you appreciate being independent.

Daily Inspiration

To live a life of gratitude is to open our eyes to the countless ways in which we are supported by the world around us.

-Gregg Krech-

DAILY GRATITUDE PRACTICE

DATE: _____

Write a few sentences describing one thing that starts with the letter U that you are grateful for.

Daily Inspiration

Gratitude is one of the sweet shortcuts to finding peace of mind and happiness inside.

-Barry Neil Kaufman-

DAILY GRATITUDE PRACTICE

DATE: _____

Write a few sentences describing one item you use daily. Reflect on how it improves your life and how thankful you are for it.

Daily Inspiration

Let us be grateful to the people who make us happy; they are the charming gardeners who make our souls blossom.

-Marcel Proust-

DAILY GRATITUDE PRACTICE

DATE: _____

Write a few sentences describing which 3 strengths you are thankful for having.

Daily Inspiration

Gratitude doesn't change the scenery. It merely washes clean the glass you look through so you can clearly see the colors.

-Richelle E. Goodrich-

DAILY GRATITUDE PRACTICE

DATE: _____

Write a few sentences describing one thing that starts with the letter V that you are grateful for.

Daily Inspiration

It is through the gratitude for the present moment that the spiritual dimension of life opens up.

-Eckhart Tolle-

DAILY GRATITUDE PRACTICE

DATE: _____

Write a few sentences describing how much you appreciate identifying with your *Myers–Briggs* personality type.

Daily Inspiration

The more you use gratitude, the stronger it grows, and the more power you have to use it on your behalf.

-Alan Cohen-

DAILY GRATITUDE PRACTICE

DATE: _____

Write a few sentences describing something you are grateful to have learned in school.

Daily Inspiration

Whatever you appreciate and give thanks for will increase in your life.

-Sanaya Roman-

DAILY GRATITUDE PRACTICE

DATE: _____

Write a few sentences describing one thing that starts with the letter **W** that you are grateful for.

Daily Inspiration

When you are grateful – when you can see what you have – you unlock blessings to flow in your life.

-Suze Orman-

DAILY GRATITUDE PRACTICE

DATE: _____

Write a few sentences describing how grateful you are for your best friend.

Daily Inspiration

If the only prayer you ever say in your entire life is *thank you*, it will be enough.

-Meister Eckhart-

DAILY GRATITUDE PRACTICE

DATE: _____

Write a few sentences describing how grateful you are to be alive and one goal you hope to accomplish throughout the week.

Daily Inspiration

It's up to us to choose contentment and thankfulness now. We don't have to have everything perfect to be happy.

-Joanna Gaines-

DAILY GRATITUDE PRACTICE

DATE: _____

Write a few sentences describing one thing that starts with the letter X that you are grateful for.

Daily Inspiration

When you are grateful, an invisible blanket of peace covers you, it makes you glow, it makes you happy, strong, warm.

-Om Swami-

DAILY GRATITUDE PRACTICE

DATE: _____

Write a few sentences describing three basic needs you are thankful you can afford.

Daily Inspiration

Start bringing gratitude to your experiences, instead of waiting for a positive experience in order to feel grateful.

-Marelisa Fábrega-

DAILY GRATITUDE PRACTICE

DATE: _____

Write a few sentences describing an artist, actor or musician you are grateful for.

Daily Inspiration

The essence of all beautiful art is gratitude.

-Friedrich Nietzsche-

DAILY GRATITUDE PRACTICE

DATE: _____

Write a few sentences describing one thing that starts with the letter Y that you are grateful for.

Daily Inspiration

If you want to find happiness, find gratitude.

-Steve Maraboli-

DAILY GRATITUDE PRACTICE

DATE: _____

Write a few sentences describing something you are grateful to have learned as an adult.

Daily Inspiration

Gratitude is an essential part of being present. When you go deeply into the present, gratitude arises spontaneously.

-Eckhart Tolle-

DAILY GRATITUDE PRACTICE

DATE: _____

Write a few sentences describing one person who is no longer part of your life that you are thankful to have let go.

Daily Inspiration

Gratitude in advance is the most powerful creative force in the universe.

-Neale Donald Walsch-

DAILY GRATITUDE PRACTICE

DATE: _____

Write a few sentences describing one thing that starts with the letter Z that you are grateful for.

Daily Inspiration

Gratitude is a direct way out of comparison.

-Robyn Conley Downs-

DAILY GRATITUDE PRACTICE

DATE: _____

Write a few sentences describing something that happened during the week that you are grateful for.

Daily Inspiration

The more that we feel grateful in our lives, the more joy we're able to feel and the more fulfilled we're able to feel.

-Miranda Anderson-

DAILY GRATITUDE PRACTICE

DATE: _____

Write a few sentences describing what flavor you are most grateful for being able to taste.

Daily Inspiration

If all you did was just look for things to appreciate, you would live a joyous, spectacular life.

-Abraham Hicks-

DAILY GRATITUDE PRACTICE

DATE: _____

Write a few sentences describing something you appreciate about your height.

Daily Inspiration

Joy is what happens to us when we allow ourselves to recognize how good things really are.

-Marianne Williamson-

DAILY GRATITUDE PRACTICE

DATE: _____

Write a few sentences describing something you appreciate about your weight.

Daily Inspiration

Gratitude puts the mind at ease about everything around.

-Om Swami-

DAILY GRATITUDE PRACTICE

DATE: _____

Write a few sentences describing an inspirational writer whose work you are grateful to have read.

Daily Inspiration

When you are alive with joy, gratitude, and genuine interest in others, you are your most beautiful. Remember that.

-Brendon Burchard-

DAILY GRATITUDE PRACTICE

DATE: _____

Write a few sentences describing something you appreciate about your local government.

Daily Inspiration

Focus on staying in the moment, on being grateful for where you are today.

-S. McNutt-

DAILY GRATITUDE PRACTICE

DATE: _____

Write a few sentences describing one thing inside your purse or wallet you are grateful for.

Daily Inspiration

I don't have to chase extraordinary moments to find happiness- it's right in front...if I'm paying attention & practicing gratitude.

-Brené Brown-

DAILY GRATITUDE PRACTICE

DATE: _____

Write a few sentences describing one thing you appreciate about Spring.

Daily Inspiration

Give thanks for unknown blessings already on their way.

-Native American Proverb-

DAILY GRATITUDE PRACTICE

DATE: _____

Write a few sentences describing one thing you appreciate about Summer.

Daily Inspiration

Gratitude is the appreciation of things that are not deserved, earned or demanded–those wonderful things we take for granted.

-Renée Paule-

DAILY GRATITUDE PRACTICE

DATE: _____

Write a few sentences describing one thing you appreciate about Autumn.

Daily Inspiration

Showing gratitude is one of the simplest yet most powerful things humans can do for each other.

-Randy Pausch-

DAILY GRATITUDE PRACTICE

DATE: _____

Write a few sentences describing one thing you appreciate about Winter.

Daily Inspiration

It is necessary to cultivate the habit of being grateful for every good thing that comes to you, and to give thanks continuously.

-Wallace D. Wattles-

DAILY GRATITUDE PRACTICE

DATE: _____

Write a few sentences describing 12 things, one for each month of the year, you are grateful for.

Daily Inspiration

As we express our gratitude, we must never forget that the highest appreciation is not to utter words, but to live by them.

-John F. Kennedy-

LATINAS 100

a Adriana Rosales Brand

DAILY PLANNER

DAILY PLANNER

DATE:

My intention for the day: ....

TO DO TODAY

- ☐ _____
- ☐ _____
- ☐ _____
- ☐ _____
- ☐ _____
- ☐ _____
- ☐ _____
- ☐ _____
- ☐ _____

NOTES & DOODLES

WELLNESS CHECK-IN

How am I feeling today?	What am I grateful for?	How will I take care of myself?

"The backbone of success is hard work, determination, good planning, and perseverance."

DAILY PLANNER

DATE:

My intention for the day: _____

TO DO TODAY

- ☐ _____
- ☐ _____
- ☐ _____
- ☐ _____
- ☐ _____
- ☐ _____
- ☐ _____
- ☐ _____
- ☐ _____

NOTES & DOODLES

WELLNESS CHECK-IN

How am I feeling today?	What am I grateful for?	How will I take care of myself?

"The backbone of success is hard work, determination, good planning, and perseverance."

DAILY PLANNER

DATE:

My intention for the day:

TO DO TODAY

- ☐ _____
- ☐ _____
- ☐ _____
- ☐ _____
- ☐ _____
- ☐ _____
- ☐ _____
- ☐ _____
- ☐ _____

NOTES & DOODLES

WELLNESS CHECK-IN

How am I feeling today?	What am I grateful for?	How will I take care of myself?

"The backbone of success is hard work, determination, good planning, and perseverance."

DAILY PLANNER

DATE:

My intention for the day:

TO DO TODAY

☐ _____
☐ _____
☐ _____
☐ _____
☐ _____
☐ _____
☐ _____
☐ _____
☐ _____

NOTES & DOODLES

WELLNESS CHECK-IN

How am I feeling today?	What am I grateful for?	How will I take care of myself?

"The backbone of success is hard work, determination, good planning, and perseverance."

DAILY PLANNER

DATE:

My intention for the day:

TO DO TODAY

- [ ] _____
- [ ] _____
- [ ] _____
- [ ] _____
- [ ] _____
- [ ] _____
- [ ] _____
- [ ] _____
- [ ] _____

NOTES & DOODLES

WELLNESS CHECK-IN

How am I feeling today?	What am I grateful for?	How will I take care of myself?

"The backbone of success is hard work, determination, good planning, and perseverance."

DAILY PLANNER

DATE:

My intention for the day:

TO DO TODAY

☐ _____
☐ _____
☐ _____
☐ _____
☐ _____
☐ _____
☐ _____
☐ _____
☐ _____

NOTES & DOODLES

WELLNESS CHECK-IN

How am I feeling today?	*What am I grateful for?*	*How will I take care of myself?*

"The backbone of success is hard work, determination, good planning, and perseverance."

DAILY PLANNER

DATE:

My intention for the day:

TO DO TODAY

- [ ] _____
- [ ] _____
- [ ] _____
- [ ] _____
- [ ] _____
- [ ] _____
- [ ] _____
- [ ] _____
- [ ] _____

NOTES & DOODLES

WELLNESS CHECK-IN

How am I feeling today?	What am I grateful for?	How will I take care of myself?

"The backbone of success is hard work, determination, good planning, and perseverance."

DAILY PLANNER

DATE:

My intention for the day:

TO DO TODAY

- ☐ _____
- ☐ _____
- ☐ _____
- ☐ _____
- ☐ _____
- ☐ _____
- ☐ _____
- ☐ _____
- ☐ _____

NOTES & DOODLES

WELLNESS CHECK-IN

How am I feeling today?	*What am I grateful for?*	*How will I take care of myself?*

"The backbone of success is hard work, determination, good planning, and perseverance."

DAILY PLANNER

DATE:

My intention for the day: ....

TO DO TODAY

☐ _____
☐ _____
☐ _____
☐ _____
☐ _____
☐ _____
☐ _____
☐ _____
☐ _____

NOTES & DOODLES

WELLNESS CHECK-IN

How am I feeling today?	What am I grateful for?	How will I take care of myself?

"The backbone of success is hard work, determination, good planning, and perseverance."

DAILY PLANNER

DATE:

My intention for the day:

TO DO TODAY

- [ ] _____
- [ ] _____
- [ ] _____
- [ ] _____
- [ ] _____
- [ ] _____
- [ ] _____
- [ ] _____
- [ ] _____

NOTES & DOODLES

WELLNESS CHECK-IN

How am I feeling today?	What am I grateful for?	How will I take care of myself?

"The backbone of success is hard work, determination, good planning, and perseverance."

DAILY PLANNER

DATE:

My intention for the day:

TO DO TODAY

- [ ] _____
- [ ] _____
- [ ] _____
- [ ] _____
- [ ] _____
- [ ] _____
- [ ] _____
- [ ] _____
- [ ] _____

NOTES & DOODLES

WELLNESS CHECK-IN

How am I feeling today?	What am I grateful for?	How will I take care of myself?

"The backbone of success is hard work, determination, good planning, and perseverance."

DAILY PLANNER

DATE:

My intention for the day:

TO DO TODAY

☐ _____
☐ _____
☐ _____
☐ _____
☐ _____
☐ _____
☐ _____
☐ _____
☐ _____

NOTES & DOODLES

WELLNESS CHECK-IN

How am I feeling today?	*What am I grateful for?*	*How will I take care of myself?*

"The backbone of success is hard work, determination, good planning, and perseverance."

DAILY PLANNER

DATE:

My intention for the day:

TO DO TODAY

- ☐ _____
- ☐ _____
- ☐ _____
- ☐ _____
- ☐ _____
- ☐ _____
- ☐ _____
- ☐ _____
- ☐ _____

NOTES & DOODLES

WELLNESS CHECK-IN

How am I feeling today?	What am I grateful for?	How will I take care of myself?

"The backbone of success is hard work, determination, good planning, and perseverance."

DAILY PLANNER

DATE:

My intention for the day:

TO DO TODAY

- ☐ _____
- ☐ _____
- ☐ _____
- ☐ _____
- ☐ _____
- ☐ _____
- ☐ _____
- ☐ _____
- ☐ _____

NOTES & DOODLES

WELLNESS CHECK-IN

How am I feeling today?	What am I grateful for?	How will I take care of myself?

"The backbone of success is hard work, determination, good planning, and perseverance."

DAILY PLANNER

DATE:

My intention for the day:

TO DO TODAY

- ☐ _____
- ☐ _____
- ☐ _____
- ☐ _____
- ☐ _____
- ☐ _____
- ☐ _____
- ☐ _____
- ☐ _____

NOTES & DOODLES

WELLNESS CHECK-IN

How am I feeling today?	What am I grateful for?	How will I take care of myself?

"The backbone of success is hard work, determination, good planning, and perseverance."

DAILY PLANNER

DATE:

My intention for the day:

TO DO TODAY

- [ ] _____
- [ ] _____
- [ ] _____
- [ ] _____
- [ ] _____
- [ ] _____
- [ ] _____
- [ ] _____
- [ ] _____

NOTES & DOODLES

WELLNESS CHECK-IN

How am I feeling today?	What am I grateful for?	How will I take care of myself?

"The backbone of success is hard work, determination, good planning, and perseverance."

DAILY PLANNER

DATE:

My intention for the day: _____

TO DO TODAY

- [ ] _____
- [ ] _____
- [ ] _____
- [ ] _____
- [ ] _____
- [ ] _____
- [ ] _____
- [ ] _____
- [ ] _____

NOTES & DOODLES

WELLNESS CHECK-IN

How am I feeling today?	What am I grateful for?	How will I take care of myself?

"The backbone of success is hard work, determination, good planning, and perseverance."

DAILY PLANNER

DATE:

My intention for the day:

TO DO TODAY

- [ ] _____
- [ ] _____
- [ ] _____
- [ ] _____
- [ ] _____
- [ ] _____
- [ ] _____
- [ ] _____
- [ ] _____

NOTES & DOODLES

WELLNESS CHECK-IN

How am I feeling today?	*What am I grateful for?*	*How will I take care of myself?*

"The backbone of success is hard work, determination, good planning, and perseverance."

DAILY PLANNER

DATE:

My intention for the day:

TO DO TODAY

- [ ] _____
- [ ] _____
- [ ] _____
- [ ] _____
- [ ] _____
- [ ] _____
- [ ] _____
- [ ] _____
- [ ] _____

NOTES & DOODLES

WELLNESS CHECK-IN

How am I feeling today?	What am I grateful for?	How will I take care of myself?

"The backbone of success is hard work, determination, good planning, and perseverance."

DAILY PLANNER

DATE:

My intention for the day:

TO DO TODAY

- [ ] _____
- [ ] _____
- [ ] _____
- [ ] _____
- [ ] _____
- [ ] _____
- [ ] _____
- [ ] _____
- [ ] _____

NOTES & DOODLES

WELLNESS CHECK-IN

How am I feeling today?	What am I grateful for?	How will I take care of myself?

"The backbone of success is hard work, determination, good planning, and perseverance."

DAILY PLANNER

DATE:

My intention for the day:

TO DO TODAY

- [ ] _____
- [ ] _____
- [ ] _____
- [ ] _____
- [ ] _____
- [ ] _____
- [ ] _____
- [ ] _____
- [ ] _____

NOTES & DOODLES

WELLNESS CHECK-IN

How am I feeling today?	What am I grateful for?	How will I take care of myself?

"The backbone of success is hard work, determination, good planning, and perseverance."

DAILY PLANNER

DATE:

My intention for the day:

TO DO TODAY

- [ ] _____
- [ ] _____
- [ ] _____
- [ ] _____
- [ ] _____
- [ ] _____
- [ ] _____
- [ ] _____
- [ ] _____

NOTES & DOODLES

WELLNESS CHECK-IN

How am I feeling today?	What am I grateful for?	How will I take care of myself?

The backbone of success is hard work, determination, good planning, and perseverance.

DAILY PLANNER

DATE:

My intention for the day: ....

TO DO TODAY

☐ _____
☐ _____
☐ _____
☐ _____
☐ _____
☐ _____
☐ _____
☐ _____
☐ _____

NOTES & DOODLES

WELLNESS CHECK-IN

How am I feeling today?	What am I grateful for?	How will I take care of myself?

"The backbone of success is hard work, determination, good planning, and perseverance."

DAILY PLANNER

DATE:

My intention for the day: _____

TO DO TODAY

- [ ] _____
- [ ] _____
- [ ] _____
- [ ] _____
- [ ] _____
- [ ] _____
- [ ] _____
- [ ] _____
- [ ] _____

NOTES & DOODLES

WELLNESS CHECK-IN

How am I feeling today?	What am I grateful for?	How will I take care of myself?

"The backbone of success is hard work, determination, good planning, and perseverance."

DAILY PLANNER

DATE:

My intention for the day: _____

TO DO TODAY

- ☐ _____
- ☐ _____
- ☐ _____
- ☐ _____
- ☐ _____
- ☐ _____
- ☐ _____
- ☐ _____
- ☐ _____

NOTES & DOODLES

WELLNESS CHECK-IN

How am I feeling today?	What am I grateful for?	How will I take care of myself?

"The backbone of success is hard work, determination, good planning, and perseverance."

DAILY PLANNER

DATE:

My intention for the day:

TO DO TODAY

- ☐ _____
- ☐ _____
- ☐ _____
- ☐ _____
- ☐ _____
- ☐ _____
- ☐ _____
- ☐ _____
- ☐ _____

NOTES & DOODLES

WELLNESS CHECK-IN

How am I feeling today?	What am I grateful for?	How will I take care of myself?

"The backbone of success is hard work, determination, good planning, and perseverance."

DAILY PLANNER

DATE:

My intention for the day:

TO DO TODAY

- ☐ _____
- ☐ _____
- ☐ _____
- ☐ _____
- ☐ _____
- ☐ _____
- ☐ _____
- ☐ _____
- ☐ _____

NOTES & DOODLES

WELLNESS CHECK-IN

How am I feeling today?	What am I grateful for?	How will I take care of myself?

"The backbone of success is hard work, determination, good planning, and perseverance."

DAILY PLANNER

DATE:

My intention for the day:

TO DO TODAY

- [ ] _____
- [ ] _____
- [ ] _____
- [ ] _____
- [ ] _____
- [ ] _____
- [ ] _____
- [ ] _____
- [ ] _____

NOTES & DOODLES

WELLNESS CHECK-IN

How am I feeling today?	What am I grateful for?	How will I take care of myself?

"The backbone of success is hard work, determination, good planning, and perseverance."

DAILY PLANNER

DATE:

My intention for the day:

TO DO TODAY

- [ ] _____
- [ ] _____
- [ ] _____
- [ ] _____
- [ ] _____
- [ ] _____
- [ ] _____
- [ ] _____
- [ ] _____

NOTES & DOODLES

WELLNESS CHECK-IN

How am I feeling today?	What am I grateful for?	How will I take care of myself?

"The backbone of success is hard work, determination, good planning, and perseverance."

DAILY PLANNER

DATE:

My intention for the day:

TO DO TODAY

- [ ] _____
- [ ] _____
- [ ] _____
- [ ] _____
- [ ] _____
- [ ] _____
- [ ] _____
- [ ] _____
- [ ] _____

NOTES & DOODLES

WELLNESS CHECK-IN

How am I feeling today?	What am I grateful for?	How will I take care of myself?

"The backbone of success is hard work, determination, good planning, and perseverance."

LATINAS 100

WEEKLY PLANNER

weekly planner

Date:

MONDAY

TUESDAY

WEDNESDAY

THURSDAY

FRIDAY

WEEKEND

TO DO LIST

♥ _____
♥ _____
♥ _____
♥ _____
♥ _____

WORDS OF INSPIRATION

NOTES

weekly planner

Date:

MONDAY

TUESDAY

WEDNESDAY

THURSDAY

FRIDAY

WEEKEND

TO DO LIST

♥ _____
♥ _____
♥ _____
♥ _____
♥ _____

WORDS OF INSPIRATION

NOTES

weekly planner

Date:

MONDAY

TUESDAY

WEDNESDAY

THURSDAY

FRIDAY

WEEKEND

TO DO LIST

♡ _____
♡ _____
♡ _____
♡ _____
♡ _____

WORDS OF INSPIRATION

NOTES

weekly planner

Date

MONDAY

TUESDAY

WEDNESDAY

THURSDAY

FRIDAY

WEEKEND

TO DO LIST

♡ _____
♡ _____
♡ _____
♡ _____
♡ _____

WORDS OF INSPIRATION

NOTES

weekly planner

Date:

MONDAY

TUESDAY

WEDNESDAY

THURSDAY

FRIDAY

WEEKEND

TO DO LIST

♥ _____
♥ _____
♥ _____
♥ _____
♥ _____

WORDS OF INSPIRATION

NOTES

weekly planner

Date:

MONDAY

TUESDAY

WEDNESDAY

THURSDAY

FRIDAY

WEEKEND

TO DO LIST

♡ _____
♡ _____
♡ _____
♡ _____
♡ _____

WORDS OF INSPIRATION

NOTES

weekly planner

Date:

MONDAY

TUESDAY

WEDNESDAY

THURSDAY

FRIDAY

WEEKEND

TO DO LIST

♡ _____
♡ _____
♡ _____
♡ _____
♡ _____

WORDS OF INSPIRATION

NOTES

weekly planner

Date:

MONDAY

TUESDAY

WEDNESDAY

THURSDAY

FRIDAY

WEEKEND

TO DO LIST

♡ _____
♡ _____
♡ _____
♡ _____
♡ _____

WORDS OF INSPIRATION

NOTES

weekly planner

Date:

MONDAY

TUESDAY

WEDNESDAY

THURSDAY

FRIDAY

WEEKEND

TO DO LIST

♥ _____
♥ _____
♥ _____
♥ _____
♥ _____

WORDS OF INSPIRATION

NOTES

weekly planner
Date:

MONDAY

TUESDAY

WEDNESDAY

THURSDAY

FRIDAY

WEEKEND

TO DO LIST

♡ _____
♡ _____
♡ _____
♡ _____
♡ _____

WORDS OF INSPIRATION

NOTES

weekly planner

Date:

MONDAY

TUESDAY

WEDNESDAY

THURSDAY

FRIDAY

WEEKEND

TO DO LIST

WORDS OF INSPIRATION

NOTES

weekly planner

Date:

MONDAY

TUESDAY

WEDNESDAY

THURSDAY

FRIDAY

WEEKEND

TO DO LIST

♡ _____
♡ _____
♡ _____
♡ _____
♡ _____

WORDS OF INSPIRATION

NOTES

weekly planner

Date:

MONDAY

TUESDAY

WEDNESDAY

THURSDAY

FRIDAY

WEEKEND

TO DO LIST

♥ _____
♥ _____
♥ _____
♥ _____
♥ _____

WORDS OF INSPIRATION

NOTES

weekly planner

Date:

MONDAY

TUESDAY

WEDNESDAY

THURSDAY

FRIDAY

WEEKEND

TO DO LIST

♡ _____
♡ _____
♡ _____
♡ _____
♡ _____

WORDS OF INSPIRATION

NOTES

weekly planner

Date:

MONDAY

TUESDAY

WEDNESDAY

THURSDAY

FRIDAY

WEEKEND

TO DO LIST

♥ _____
♥ _____
♥ _____
♥ _____
♥ _____

WORDS OF INSPIRATION

NOTES

weekly planner

Date:

MONDAY

TUESDAY

WEDNESDAY

THURSDAY

FRIDAY

WEEKEND

TO DO LIST

♡ _____
♡ _____
♡ _____
♡ _____
♡ _____

WORDS OF INSPIRATION

NOTES

weekly planner

Date:

MONDAY

TUESDAY

WEDNESDAY

THURSDAY

FRIDAY

WEEKEND

TO DO LIST

♥ _____
♥ _____
♥ _____
♥ _____
♥ _____

WORDS OF INSPIRATION

NOTES

weekly planner

Date:

MONDAY

TUESDAY

WEDNESDAY

THURSDAY

FRIDAY

WEEKEND

TO DO LIST

♡ _____
♡ _____
♡ _____
♡ _____
♡ _____

WORDS OF INSPIRATION

NOTES

weekly planner

Date:

MONDAY

TUESDAY

WEDNESDAY

THURSDAY

FRIDAY

WEEKEND

TO DO LIST

♥ _____
♥ _____
♥ _____
♥ _____
♥ _____

WORDS OF INSPIRATION

NOTES

weekly planner

Date:

MONDAY

TUESDAY

WEDNESDAY

THURSDAY

FRIDAY

WEEKEND

TO DO LIST
♡ _____
♡ _____
♡ _____
♡ _____
♡ _____

WORDS OF INSPIRATION

NOTES

weekly planner

Date:

MONDAY

TUESDAY

WEDNESDAY

THURSDAY

FRIDAY

WEEKEND

TO DO LIST

♡ _____
♡ _____
♡ _____
♡ _____
♡ _____

WORDS OF INSPIRATION

NOTES

weekly planner

Date:

MONDAY

TUESDAY

WEDNESDAY

THURSDAY

FRIDAY

WEEKEND

TO DO LIST
♡ _____
♡ _____
♡ _____
♡ _____
♡ _____

WORDS OF INSPIRATION

NOTES

weekly planner

Date:

MONDAY

TUESDAY

WEDNESDAY

THURSDAY

FRIDAY

WEEKEND

TO DO LIST

♥ _____
♥ _____
♥ _____
♥ _____
♥ _____

WORDS OF INSPIRATION

NOTES

weekly planner

Date:

MONDAY

TUESDAY

WEDNESDAY

THURSDAY

FRIDAY

WEEKEND

TO DO LIST

♡ _____
♡ _____
♡ _____
♡ _____
♡ _____

WORDS OF INSPIRATION

NOTES

weekly planner

Date:

MONDAY

TUESDAY

WEDNESDAY

THURSDAY

FRIDAY

WEEKEND

TO DO LIST

WORDS OF INSPIRATION

NOTES

weekly planner

Date:

MONDAY

TUESDAY

WEDNESDAY

THURSDAY

FRIDAY

WEEKEND

TO DO LIST

♡ _____
♡ _____
♡ _____
♡ _____
♡ _____

WORDS OF INSPIRATION

NOTES

weekly planner
Date

MONDAY

TUESDAY

WEDNESDAY

THURSDAY

FRIDAY

WEEKEND

TO DO LIST
♡ _____
♡ _____
♡ _____
♡ _____
♡ _____

WORDS OF INSPIRATION

NOTES

weekly planner

Date:

MONDAY

TUESDAY

WEDNESDAY

THURSDAY

FRIDAY

WEEKEND

TO DO LIST
♡ _____
♡ _____
♡ _____
♡ _____
♡ _____

WORDS OF INSPIRATION

NOTES

weekly planner
Date:

MONDAY

TUESDAY

WEDNESDAY

THURSDAY

FRIDAY

WEEKEND

TO DO LIST

♡ _____
♡ _____
♡ _____
♡ _____
♡ _____

WORDS OF INSPIRATION

NOTES

weekly planner

Date:

MONDAY

TUESDAY

WEDNESDAY

THURSDAY

FRIDAY

WEEKEND

TO DO LIST

♡ _____
♡ _____
♡ _____
♡ _____
♡ _____

WORDS OF INSPIRATION

NOTES

weekly planner

Date:

MONDAY

TUESDAY

WEDNESDAY

THURSDAY

FRIDAY

WEEKEND

TO DO LIST

♡ _____
♡ _____
♡ _____
♡ _____
♡ _____

WORDS OF INSPIRATION

NOTES

weekly planner

Date:

MONDAY

TUESDAY

WEDNESDAY

THURSDAY

FRIDAY

WEEKEND

TO DO LIST

♥ _____
♥ _____
♥ _____
♥ _____
♥ _____

WORDS OF INSPIRATION

NOTES

weekly planner

Date:

MONDAY

TUESDAY

WEDNESDAY

THURSDAY

FRIDAY

WEEKEND

TO DO LIST

♥ _____
♥ _____
♥ _____
♥ _____
♥ _____

WORDS OF INSPIRATION

NOTES

weekly planner

Date:

MONDAY

TUESDAY

WEDNESDAY

THURSDAY

FRIDAY

WEEKEND

TO DO LIST

♡ _____
♡ _____
♡ _____
♡ _____
♡ _____

WORDS OF INSPIRATION

NOTES

weekly planner

Date:

MONDAY

TUESDAY

WEDNESDAY

THURSDAY

FRIDAY

WEEKEND

TO DO LIST

♥ _____
♥ _____
♥ _____
♥ _____
♥ _____

WORDS OF INSPIRATION

NOTES

weekly planner

Date:

MONDAY

TUESDAY

WEDNESDAY

THURSDAY

FRIDAY

WEEKEND

TO DO LIST

♡ _____
♡ _____
♡ _____
♡ _____
♡ _____

WORDS OF INSPIRATION

NOTES

weekly planner

Date:

MONDAY

TUESDAY

WEDNESDAY

THURSDAY

FRIDAY

WEEKEND

TO DO LIST

♡ _____
♡ _____
♡ _____
♡ _____
♡ _____

WORDS OF INSPIRATION

NOTES

weekly planner

Date:

MONDAY

TUESDAY

WEDNESDAY

THURSDAY

FRIDAY

WEEKEND

TO DO LIST

WORDS OF INSPIRATION

NOTES

weekly planner

Date:

MONDAY

TUESDAY

WEDNESDAY

THURSDAY

FRIDAY

WEEKEND

TO DO LIST

♥ _____
♥ _____
♥ _____
♥ _____
♥ _____

WORDS OF INSPIRATION

NOTES

weekly planner

Date:

MONDAY

TUESDAY

WEDNESDAY

THURSDAY

FRIDAY

WEEKEND

TO DO LIST

♡ _____
♡ _____
♡ _____
♡ _____
♡ _____

WORDS OF INSPIRATION

NOTES

weekly planner

Date:

MONDAY

TUESDAY

WEDNESDAY

THURSDAY

FRIDAY

WEEKEND

TO DO LIST

♡ _____
♡ _____
♡ _____
♡ _____
♡ _____

WORDS OF INSPIRATION

NOTES

weekly planner

Date:

MONDAY

TUESDAY

WEDNESDAY

THURSDAY

FRIDAY

WEEKEND

TO DO LIST

♡ _____
♡ _____
♡ _____
♡ _____
♡ _____

WORDS OF INSPIRATION

NOTES

weekly planner

Date:

MONDAY

TUESDAY

WEDNESDAY

THURSDAY

FRIDAY

WEEKEND

TO DO LIST

♡ _____
♡ _____
♡ _____
♡ _____
♡ _____

WORDS OF INSPIRATION

NOTES

weekly planner

Date:

MONDAY

TUESDAY

WEDNESDAY

THURSDAY

FRIDAY

WEEKEND

TO DO LIST
♡ _____
♡ _____
♡ _____
♡ _____
♡ _____

WORDS OF INSPIRATION

NOTES

weekly planner

Date:

MONDAY

TUESDAY

WEDNESDAY

THURSDAY

FRIDAY

WEEKEND

TO DO LIST

♥ _____
♥ _____
♥ _____
♥ _____
♥ _____

WORDS OF INSPIRATION

NOTES

weekly planner

Date:

MONDAY

TUESDAY

WEDNESDAY

THURSDAY

FRIDAY

WEEKEND

TO DO LIST

- ♡ _____
- ♡ _____
- ♡ _____
- ♡ _____
- ♡ _____

WORDS OF INSPIRATION

NOTES

weekly planner

Date:

MONDAY

TUESDAY

WEDNESDAY

THURSDAY

FRIDAY

WEEKEND

TO DO LIST

♥ _____
♥ _____
♥ _____
♥ _____
♥ _____

WORDS OF INSPIRATION

NOTES

weekly planner
Date:

MONDAY

TUESDAY

WEDNESDAY

THURSDAY

FRIDAY

WEEKEND

TO DO LIST
♡ _____
♡ _____
♡ _____
♡ _____
♡ _____

WORDS OF INSPIRATION

NOTES

weekly planner

Date:

MONDAY

TUESDAY

WEDNESDAY

THURSDAY

FRIDAY

WEEKEND

TO DO LIST

♥ _____
♥ _____
♥ _____
♥ _____
♥ _____

WORDS OF INSPIRATION

NOTES

DOTTED SHEETS

BUDGET SHEETS

LATINAS 100

Income

Dates _____

Income Source	Budgeted	Amount	Remaining Income	Amount
	$	$	Total Income	$
	$	$	Total Expenses	$
	$	$	Remaining	$
Total	$	$	Total	$

Expenses

Expense	Budgeted	Amount	Expense	Budgeted	Amount
	$	$		$	$
	$	$		$	$
	$	$		$	$
	$	$		$	$
	$	$		$	$
	$	$		$	$
	$	$		$	$
	$	$		$	$
	$	$		$	$
Total	$	$	Total	$	$

Debt Repayment

Creditor	Balance	Paid
	$	$
	$	$
	$	$

Savings

Account	Goal	Amount
	$	$
	$	$

Income

Dates _____

Income Source	Budgeted	Amount	Remaining Income	Amount
	$	$	Total Income	$
	$	$	Total Expenses	$
	$	$	Remaining	$
Total	$	$	Total	$

Expenses

Expense	Budgeted	Amount	Expense	Budgeted	Amount
	$	$		$	$
	$	$		$	$
	$	$		$	$
	$	$		$	$
	$	$		$	$
	$	$		$	$
	$	$		$	$
	$	$		$	$
	$	$		$	$
Total	$	$	Total	$	$

Debt Repayment

Creditor	Balance	Paid
	$	$
	$	$
	$	$

Savings

Account	Goal	Amount
	$	$
	$	$

Income

Dates _____

Income Source	Budgeted	Amount	Remaining Income	Amount
	$	$	Total Income	$
	$	$	Total Expenses	$
	$	$	Remaining	$
Total	$	$	Total	$

Expenses

Expense	Budgeted	Amount	Expense	Budgeted	Amount
	$	$		$	$
	$	$		$	$
	$	$		$	$
	$	$		$	$
	$	$		$	$
	$	$		$	$
	$	$		$	$
	$	$		$	$
	$	$		$	$
Total	$	$	Total	$	$

Debt Repayment

Creditor	Balance	Paid
	$	$
	$	$
	$	$

Savings

Account	Goal	Amount
	$	$
	$	$

Income

Dates _____

Income Source	Budgeted	Amount		Remaining Income	Amount
	$	$		Total Income	$
	$	$		Total Expenses	$
	$	$		Remaining	$
Total	$	$		Total	$

Expenses

Expense	Budgeted	Amount	Expense	Budgeted	Amount
	$	$		$	$
	$	$		$	$
	$	$		$	$
	$	$		$	$
	$	$		$	$
	$	$		$	$
	$	$		$	$
	$	$		$	$
	$	$		$	$
Total	$	$	Total	$	$

Debt Repayment

Creditor	Balance	Paid
	$	$
	$	$
	$	$

Savings

Account	Goal	Amount
	$	$
	$	$

Income

Dates _____

Income Source	Budgeted	Amount	Remaining Income	Amount
	$	$	Total Income	$
	$	$	Total Expenses	$
	$	$	Remaining	$
Total	$	$	Total	$

Expenses

Expense	Budgeted	Amount	Expense	Budgeted	Amount
	$	$		$	$
	$	$		$	$
	$	$		$	$
	$	$		$	$
	$	$		$	$
	$	$		$	$
	$	$		$	$
	$	$		$	$
	$	$		$	$
Total	$	$	Total	$	$

Debt Repayment

Creditor	Balance	Paid
	$	$
	$	$
	$	$

Savings

Account	Goal	Amount
	$	$
	$	$

Income

Dates _____

Income Source	Budgeted	Amount	Remaining Income	Amount
	$	$	Total Income	$
	$	$	Total Expenses	$
	$	$	Remaining	$
Total	$	$	Total	$

Expenses

Expense	Budgeted	Amount	Expense	Budgeted	Amount
	$	$		$	$
	$	$		$	$
	$	$		$	$
	$	$		$	$
	$	$		$	$
	$	$		$	$
	$	$		$	$
	$	$		$	$
	$	$		$	$
Total	$	$	Total	$	$

Debt Repayment

Creditor	Balance	Paid
	$	$
	$	$
	$	$

Savings

Account	Goal	Amount
	$	$
	$	$

Income

Dates _____

Income Source	Budgeted	Amount	Remaining Income	Amount
	$	$	Total Income	$
	$	$	Total Expenses	$
	$	$	Remaining	$
Total	$	$	Total	$

Expenses

Expense	Budgeted	Amount	Expense	Budgeted	Amount
	$	$		$	$
	$	$		$	$
	$	$		$	$
	$	$		$	$
	$	$		$	$
	$	$		$	$
	$	$		$	$
	$	$		$	$
	$	$		$	$
Total	$	$	Total	$	$

Debt Repayment

Creditor	Balance	Paid
	$	$
	$	$
	$	$

Savings

Account	Goal	Amount
	$	$
	$	$

Income

Dates _____

Income Source	Budgeted	Amount
	$	$
	$	$
	$	$
Total	$	$

Remaining Income	Amount
Total Income	$
Total Expenses	$
Remaining	$
Total	$

Expenses

Expense	Budgeted	Amount
	$	$
	$	$
	$	$
	$	$
	$	$
	$	$
	$	$
	$	$
	$	$
Total	$	$

Expense	Budgeted	Amount
	$	$
	$	$
	$	$
	$	$
	$	$
	$	$
	$	$
	$	$
	$	$
Total	$	$

Debt Repayment

Creditor	Balance	Paid
	$	$
	$	$
	$	$

Savings

Account	Goal	Amount
	$	$
	$	$

Income

Dates _____

Income Source	Budgeted	Amount		Remaining Income	Amount
	$	$		Total Income	$
	$	$		Total Expenses	$
	$	$		Remaining	$
Total	$	$		Total	$

Expenses

Expense	Budgeted	Amount		Expense	Budgeted	Amount
	$	$			$	$
	$	$			$	$
	$	$			$	$
	$	$			$	$
	$	$			$	$
	$	$			$	$
	$	$			$	$
	$	$			$	$
	$	$			$	$
Total	$	$		Total	$	$

Debt Repayment

Creditor	Balance	Paid
	$	$
	$	$
	$	$

Savings

Account	Goal	Amount
	$	$
	$	$

Income

Dates _____

Income Source	Budgeted	Amount	Remaining Income	Amount
	$	$	Total Income	$
	$	$	Total Expenses	$
	$	$	Remaining	$
Total	$	$	Total	$

Expenses

Expense	Budgeted	Amount	Expense	Budgeted	Amount
	$	$		$	$
	$	$		$	$
	$	$		$	$
	$	$		$	$
	$	$		$	$
	$	$		$	$
	$	$		$	$
	$	$		$	$
	$	$		$	$
Total	$	$	Total	$	$

Debt Repayment

Creditor	Balance	Paid
	$	$
	$	$
	$	$

Savings

Account	Goal	Amount
	$	$
	$	$

Adriana Rosales

Adriana Rosales is a member of the Forbes Coaches Council, John Maxwell certified speaker, HeartMath® Certified and an educator of personal resilience and self-regulation. Adriana mentors business professionals on the six core HeartMath® tools and techniques for stress reduction & impacts executives at her high-level seminars with John Maxwell curriculum.

She helps women and men publish for the first time for free in her yearly anthologies. Submit at 800-1000 word essay about inspiring the next generation by leaving your legacy. All the details here:
www.Latinas100.com

Rosales Mavericks Publishing Studio
1180 N. Town Center Suite #100
Las Vegas, Nevada 89144
www.Latinas100.com
www.Adriana.Company/PublishingStudio

Made in the USA
Middletown, DE
03 August 2023